Weathered Man

A book of journal poems

Weathered Man

A book of journal poems by

Alan Basting

© 2025 Alan Basting. All rights reserved.
This material may not be reproduced in any form, published,
reprinted, recorded, performed, broadcast,
rewritten, or redistributed without
the explicit permission of Alan Basting.
All such actions are strictly prohibited by law.

Cover design by Shay Culligan
Cover image by Todd Trapani
Author photo by Cassie Basting

ISBN: 978-1-63980-762-8

Kelsay Books
502 South 1040 East, A-119
American Fork, Utah 84003
Kelsaybooks.com

This book is dedicated to grandparents, everywhere

Contents

Preface	13
June 26	15
June 29	16
June 30	17
July 1	18
July 2	19
July 4th	20
July 7	21
July 8	22
July 9	23
July 10	24
July 11	25
July 13	26
July 14	27
July 16	28
July 17	29
July 18	30
July 18	31
July 19	32
July 20	33
July 21	34
July 22	35
July 23	36
July 26	37
July 27	38
July 28	39
July 30	40
August 2	41
August 3	42
August 3, #2	43
August 4	44
August 4, #2	45

August 5	46
August 6	47
August 7	48
August 8	49
August 10	50
August 15	51
August 17	52
August 18	53
August 22	54
August 24	55
August 26	56
August 27	57
August 30	58
August 30, #2	59
September 6	60
September 7	61
September 8	62
September 10	63
September 12	64
September 14	65
September 15	66
September 16	67
September 17	68
September 20	69
September 21	70
September 24	71
September 25	72
September 28	73
September 30	74
October 1	75
October 3	76
October 4	77
October 5	78

October 12	79
October 13	80
October 14	81
October 17	82
October 20	83
October 24	84
October 26	85
October 27	86
October 29	87
October 30	88
October 31	89
November 1	90
November 2	91
November 3	92
November 4	93
November 5	94
November 6	95
November 11	96
November 17	97
November 18	98
November 19	99
November 21	100
November 24	101
November 25	102
November 28–30	103
December 2	104
December 7	105
December 8	106
December 10	107
December 16	108
December 17	109
December 18	110
December 19	111

December 21	112
December 24	113
December 26	114
December 27	115
December 31	116

Preface

I began these journal poems during the early years (2021) of the Covid-19 pandemic, and while the time frames them, somewhat, I rarely alluded to the ongoing crisis, since I had plenty of my own troubles to sort through. To begin with, living in relative isolation, I did not feel the high anxiety experienced by those in populated areas who were forced to change normal social behaviors and maintain masked distances. A home in the Manistee National Forest had its advantages during the pandemic; I already was isolated by distance from old friends and relatives, and my children were past school age. The distance, however, did not exempt me from effects the virus had on the larger social fabric of community, State, and nation.

The format for these poems was inspired by Ted Kooser's volume, *Winter Morning Walks, 100 Postcards to Jim Harrison,* and the credit for the structure goes to Kooser whose writing I greatly admire. In *Weathered Man,* I let the weather for the day open the door to each of the poems. Sometimes the weather and the poems were related, and other times, not so much. Many of the poems revolve around the immediate family, and what we used to call *local color.* And, while I escaped the dark and invasive clouds of the Covid virus, I could not outrun the environmental and emotional storms surrounding me.

Finally, special thanks to Marilyn Hedgpeth for suggesting the title.

June 26

Overcast with rain, high 70s

Daylilies lift
their yellow cups
toasting rain
and its refreshment.
Delighted
with the salute
and party faces
the host
fills their flutes—
again, and again.

June 29

Oyster gray skies and muggy with rain

After thumb-squishing
a thousand red and blue
dot-lined caterpillars,
my mood and mind
are sullen as pavement.

But I am revived
by a garden walk
with my sidekick-grandson:
roses and begonias,
blossoms exploding
(scarlet, orange,
flaming yellow)
celebrating
an early 4th of July.

June 30

After days of rain
Sun and patchy nimbus clouds

Eight-five degrees and humid
but I slide thick, rubber gloves
over sweating arms and hands,
protection from the pillars'
poisonous setae. The Gypsy-moth
infestation has left us
with hundreds of thousands,
maybe a million, oak, maple,
poplar, White pine and
Douglas fir defoliated,
stripped to the bleak
and empty spindles
of deep winter.

July 1

Breezy and full sun
with powder blue skies

Dreaming of a woman
not my wife
I wake this morning
excited, wondering
What was that all about?
I hop on my lawn tractor
to figure things out,
tidying up greenery
and my thoughts. But
I may have to mow my way
to Kansas for an answer.

July 2

A baby blue afternoon in the 80s

Old willows and maples
swirl a dark, green paisley shadow
on the lawn. And beyond, sun
stretches on a thick, grass carpet,
a sleeping yellow cat. Propped
in bed with an afternoon coffee,
my own legs stretched
and relaxed, I am content
to eat cookies and sip, growing
no wiser by the minute.

July 4th

Full sun and plenty of heat
through a thin gauze of clouds

Fuzzy Meyer died this morning,
the 4th, a perfect day
for his passing. American
Family Hero grounded
in work and beliefs simple
as a flat-top haircut.
His rebuilt '65 red & white
Mustang convertible
shined as his pride and joy,
parade perfect.
During evening fireworks,
as if to celebrate his passing,
fireflies confetti our
darkened woods
outdueling overhead bursts
of aerial gunpowder.

July 7

Hot, clear skies, 90

Heavy thunderstorms overnight
clear the morning air.
A blistering sun now
shoves shady clouds
over the horizon's cliff
for good measure.
Joy a-plenty over the years,
we're celebrating our daughter's
birthday, pie and ice cream
for everyone. Blooming
with generosity, I may give
even my adversarial squirrels
a pass on the bird feeder
for a dinner of suet and seed.

July 8

Dingy gray with drizzle, 80s

Cycling a rise in pavement
along 15 Mile, I spy the largest
black, bird-shape I've ever seen
crouched along road's edge—
an adult eagle scavenging, maybe?
Pedaling closer, the silhouette lifts
its head and separates: two vultures,
one behind, enlarging the other.
Now four black eyes glare at me,
my approach disturbing breakfast.
They loop away long enough
to allow my passage, then resettle . . .
a wake of vultures, shadows
over a feast.

July 9

Sea blue skies, sunny and cool, 70s

The lake's a carpet of diamonds,
undulations pushed by a light
blue breeze, air crisp
yet heated with strong sun.
Looking shoreward from my rowboat
Gypsy moths have blossomed,
a thousand white-winged flowers
among stripped branches
of oak and birch, heart-sickening
for a tree lover, who winces
receiving a black-branched
bouquet of bare sticks.

July 10

Partly cloudy with occasional sun, 70s

All these birthdays
stuffed in my pocket,
why can't I write
something simple
and grounded . . . something
to touch millions.
Better yet, something
that might halt these two
hummingbirds
from darting and charging,
doing their best
to stab each other
with sabery beaks.

July 11

Azure skies, mild temps, mid 70s

Two trays on the day's scale
teeter for balance:
Gypsy-moth infestation
heavy as bad dreams; and
a nearly toothless smile
from a six-year-old tomboy
splashing in shallows
with my grandson,
beaming up at me,
blue eyes shining, asking
What's your name?
I'm Charise!

July 13

*Early morning rain, followed by
a sunny 75, traveling in the UP (vacation)*

Deep-fried whitefish,
delicious. A sunny blonde
waitress from Cut River
whispers the *special* numbers
culled from her receipts—twice
in the same afternoon
her checks have totaled
18.06 and 46.07, mine, one
of the latter. She nudges me . . .
use the numbers—
buy some tickets!
you could be a big winner.

I tell her the whitefish
was first prize! She chuckles
and clucks her tongue,
You need to try the baked apple
with ice cream, she tells me.
And, Oh, how I love Cut River.

July 14

*Sunny and humid, then
thunderstorms and cooling*

Damsel flies from Lake Michigan
"Organizing," hundreds of them
gathered and aligned on screens
outside the restaurant. They want in
and a seat at the table! Sizzling
burgers and whitefish
incite buzz riots
and a rattling of screens.

July 16

High pressure, bright blue skies
all day, 82

Menominee, a town name
from a children's storybook
like Bonomo's or Blimpy Bay.
A half mile stretch of clean
brick-refreshed facades.
Healthy geranium baskets,
pink, white and red,
hang from neat, black
lamp posts.

Across the river's dividing bridge,
Marinette: a town of tough
boat builders, reconditioners
of Coast Guard cutters
framed to handle great waves
hurled up by an angry
Lake Michigan. A bar
for beer and burgers
on every corner,
neighborhoods crafted
for big men, big beards,
and bigger women
from Wisconsin.

July 17

High blue skies, low humidity, 85

At a picnic table close
to the big lake's stony shoreline
I'm taking early morning
Communion, with coffee;
suddenly three
huge geese shoot past,
eye level, startling me.
Streakers . . . flapping, honking
or laughing,
I can't be sure.

July 18

A hazed blue and red-orange sunset,
85 degrees

Forest fires in Canada smear
the UP's sky with smoke.
Heading home from vacation
we're forced to retreat
at Epoufette Bay and double back
to a campground and beach
at Hog Island. The Mackinaw Bridge,
massive artery from Michigan's mitten
to its Upper Peninsula, and pride
of the state's North . . . CLOSED,
shut down completely
by a phone call—a bomb threat,
a stand-still holdup
forced by allegations of bomb sticks
hung from stanchions
deep under cold, cold water.
Only a shallow, whispery threat,
but such a long way down
to grave, shimmering waters
for bridge painters
and innocent travelers
who might happen
to be crossing . . .
just then.

July 18

(later that evening)

Camping in woods near a beach,
shallow with sippy waves, we wade
and wait for the bridge (Big Mack),
a helpless strongman
of concrete and steel,
to get a clean bill of health
from diving inspectors,
doctors of preventive detonation.

July 19

Smokey skies, 86, with humidity,
Back on the road

Crossing the bridge, we connect
eyes with the paint crew
who swing over rail barriers
to reach the bridge's lower levels,
support towers rising overhead
like skyscrapers, the blue
and glistening floor below
certain death should they fall.
They smile and wave back
nonchalantly
at our passing.

July 20

Pearly skies, hot and humid, 90

Vacation's over. At Indian River
good food is replaced
with bad nachos.

Rolling into my drive
and cutting the truck's
rumbling engine—

silence.

Time
to cut grass,
recalibrate, and return
to a workweek
filled with thankful,
pensive mowing.

July 21

Cooler this morning, silver haze

I'm awake but
bed-lazy, tired from travel.
Watching television after
a week away, it's clear
World News hasn't missed me
or noticed my vacation.
Squirrels at the bird feeders
are greedy and annoying
as they were a week ago.

July 22

*Overcast, mid-70s, cooling breeze
across the lake*

Bees forgive me
your accidental deaths.
I wish I could detour
my mowing paths,
avoid your clover
landing pads, but they're
everywhere. I promise
no chemical interventions,
but please,
remove your bee-dance curse:
two finches in four days
breaking themselves
against my windows.
This web of sadness
must end.

July 23

*More gloomy clouds, afternoon rain,
muggy 85*

Fifth-wheel scrubbed and washed,
then rain and rolling thunder.
Pleased the soapy work
is finished, I am thankful
for the 10,000 drops . . .
an effortless rinse
from a clean, sudden downpour,
and a four-year-old
rain dancing
in his T-rex underpants.

July 26

Periwinkle sky, humid, warming to 90

Two days hovering
over cycle parts and tools,
probing into nuts and bolts
reassembling a rear wheel,
brake calipers, a tricky
master cylinder, till I've
made it whole again,
the skeleton's bones put back
in place, no extra parts haunting
my re-creation. Now, on to
new fluids, life blood of this
save-my-ass-stop-me-quick system:
no air-bubble-mush-cells allowed.

July 27

Clear skies, high temps, breezy 84

My wife's greenhouse:
a glass ship sailing
over lakeside grasses.
Passengers: pickle cukes,
cherry tomatoes, Big Boys
and Early Girls, warmed
and climbing into sunny days.
First fruits hanging behind windows:
ripening, cherub faces.

July 28

Gauzy haze, high humidity, no breeze

Dead calm. The heat
pressing down
till every pore is oozing
beads of sweat. Even
our flowers, who love summer,
wilt in discomfort.
All a poet can offer—
a cool, green word: moss,
and a chilled hand
for heat-stricken plants.
Cold tea and ice
for a melting biped
and a brimmed hat,
shade for a sweaty brain.

July 30

High clouds, wild blue,
a chilly 54 at 6 AM

End of July, waking up
chilled from an overnight plunge
in temps. Then pedaling 15 Mile Rd,
witness to amazing oaks, nearly
re-leafed after Gypsy-moth
devastation. Poplars still laboring,
pushing through summer's
highs and lows. Trees recovering:
we hope they hold second
leaves longer, deeper
into fall's cool nights
and early winter.

August 2

Smoke-hazy, sunny but cool, low 70s

Visited by a local bear
disgusted with our seed-poor
buffet. She's flipped
the storage bench
on its backside, left
the birdfeeder's wood
claw-mangled and chewed,
a wrought-iron shepherd's hook
bent to a U-shaped frown.

With an exit flourish, she swatted
our twinkling solar lamps
into a grass-green heaven,
where they glistened
like wounded stars.

August 3

Blue and cool, low 70s,
High 40s overnight

An odd summer night
when temps dropped suddenly.
Wild ferns in roadside ditches
spread rust-edged fronds,
and Black-eyed Susan's sway
in the berm. But August's hardy army
of Goldenrod marches across fields
to overrun and choke-out
the Susan beauties.

      *

Yesterday I heard a cicada: one,
sawing in the back yard,
then discovered him clinging
to our greenhouse door.
His song says, he knows
what's coming;
I only wish I did.

August 3, #2

Cycling south on Highway 37
I scratch my bare forehead, maybe
gnats or tiny spiders, but I see no
insect scraps or crushed bugs
smeared on the tips of my gloves;
then I remember no-see-ums,
and I'm instantly back in Scotland,
the Highlands, walking into a cloud
of torture-grade no-see-ums,
jigging and slapping my way back
to refuge in a van, slamming
the door quickly . . . glaring out
at their "nothingness," itchy rashes
rising on my face and forearms.

August 4

*Leaden skies and humid, temps rising
into the high 80s*

Waking to mist and fog,
dew flecks stipple the window screen,
droplets hanging from nylon lace.
I feel meshed in an old Japanese painting:
tips of trees rise like fog-hazed
mountains on the far shoreline,
ragged shadows and domed foreheads
peeking over clouds. "Where
are my silk robes and samurai blade?"
I ask my wife, who only chuckles,
grasping the essence
of our window's canvas.

August 4, #2

Morning's foggy veil
left me wondering: Can anything
more than thoughts
pass freely through
our cloud-wisp fabric
of space and time?

Other spirit-lives, maybe?

August 5

Hazy, sunny, humid 80s, again

Barely visible through mist,
the creekside Martin house
rises through fog,
a lighthouse turret.

Dipping and swooping up,
circling the shrouded house,
Martins blip in and out
of visibility, as if tethered
by tiny threads to home.
A pattern familiar to me:
the bird-world version
of the 1950s atom—
feathered electrons
orbiting the core.

August 6

Cloudy drizzle, high 70s

Stepping out near the edge
of our thin woods and stream,
I startle, inadvertently,
a Great Blue Heron
perched, unusually,
on a dead branch overhead.

I've rattled his solitude,
his fishing pose
a feathered statue.

The shallow pond's surface
below him is smooth,
a rug of silver clouds
stretched flat, reflections
over water.

Avoiding a deadly beak-jab,
shadowy fish-jets dart
beneath the cloudy camouflage.

August 7

Sunny and moist, low 80s

(for Joan Griswald, R.I.P.)

At eighty-nine our neighbor's
earned the privilege
of keeping to herself: reading
at her pleasure and eating pizza,
whenever. Yesterday at the end
of a visit with my wife, she gifted us
with a cairn: a small, stacked piece
for the flower garden
bordering her home and ours.
A solid, peaceful reminder
of her presence in our lives,
an affection she has
earned, as well.

August 8

Rain early, then bright sun,
High heat and humidity

Returning in the car
from a fancy breakfast
at the golf course,
a large, three-hundred pound
black bear gallops across
the road and scrambles into forest
in front of us.

Just a wild reminder,
this is still
a hungry place to live.

August 10

Low 90s, darkening skies

No poems for two days.
Not good. Severe
thunderstorms rock evening
late into night. High winds,
big rain. Weather doing
what weather always does . . .
making more. I hope my mind
clears in the morning, and I can
follow the weather's example.

August 15

Cool and breezy, fluffy clouds
in a pool of blue

Sunday morning on a friend's
front porch, white spindled rails
trellised with morning glory,
surrounded by coneflower and
butterfly plant, fully bloomed.
Cattails along a pond's edge sway
like breeze-led dancers.

I'm a wallflower plunked
in a deck chair, with butterflies
and bees humming nearby.
Out of blue sky, the distant
softened clangs of church bells
float to a land in my ears, eyes
closed and content with the moment.

August 17

Dewy late night, cool temps

In bed I reach out to hold
the front paw of my old dog,
Tillie, wanting her to know
if night shifts suddenly
and the bed begins to spin,
she is connected . . . not alone.
And if a darkness,
or any other angel, comes calling,
I am here for her,
(even if it's me
who might need
the comforting).

August 18

Partly sunny, warm, low 80s

In contrast to the hoarse and throaty
grrrruk . . . grrrruk . . . graveled
from a heron's long neck, its flight
is elegance and slow grace,
a feathered goddess
flying across a stage,
arms outstretched
in a ballet of pure silence.

How sad for me now
to find one broken and splayed,
struck by a car and pitched
roadside, eyes wide
and surprised . . . intimidating
for scavengers, who expect
their meal to appear
lifeless.

August 22

*Evening weather clear, cool
less humidity, 79*

Yesterday a loon allowed
my pontoon to pass
closely, without diving
or lifting off. Unusual.
And I wondered:
Confused? Dazed? Certainly
not its skittish self.
My son said he saw
the same bird
pecking grass near the house.
Very unusual.

Maybe she has
a message to deliver
(from my parents
wandering the other side?)
I need to reach out . . .
open my head and heart
to this bird.

August 24

Muggy, humid, 90

Bruce couldn't make it
last night. Instead, he sent
a picture from his phone:
a glacier glistening blue,
an ice field cradled in the palms
of two surrounding peaks,
sky bright blue, and a deep
dark swath of ocean water
lapping on glacial shores . . .
Alaska.

Lucky Bruce, standing
at a ship's rail, fully
awake and peering
into a dream's blue world.

August 26

Leaden skies, humid 90s

For two days
in the steam of late August,
I have been steaming myself,
angry with the worker who drank
while he mowed weeds
along our country two-lane,
tossing empty Bud Lights
over his shoulder into grass.

I expected to find the fool's body,
toppled from his tractor
after finishing his 12-pack.
But I never found him,
dead drunk or otherwise.

So, I'm collecting his cans
and building a shrine,
a workingman's two-holer,
where others can help me
celebrate his life with shit.

August 27

Warm and ashen with light rain

Writing this morning to remove
negative thoughts, accompanying anguish
over my son's and his son's
lingering problems.
Thickened clouds and rain,
no help. Maybe it's time
for coffee and animal crackers.
Let thunder and splattering rain
wash the worst out of me.

August 30

Clear skies, cooler temps, drier weather

A Zoom meeting yesterday, kick off
for a journal's publication. Several
poets presenting work. At the end
of each reading, the audience,
framed in little Zoom squares,
clapped hands vigorously,
each one muted and silent,
e-masks firmly in place. The screen
made my grandson laugh.

August 30, #2

Another female grosbeak whacks
the porch window and dies
after dining at the copper-lidded feeder.
Between chipmunks killed
around my foundation, and songbirds
crashing into windows, I am caught
in a web of dark karma, tangled
in strands of death and liberation.
I do my best. Nurture what I can.

September 6

*Gorgeous, crystal-blue skies, low temps,
no humidity. Fall-ish*

Several days parched
without writing.
My birthday passed
amid a food-fest weekend
near Lake Michigan. A tightness
in my chest returning, I need
more exercise, fewer helpings.

Wellness and mental health
recurring themes
around our household lately.
We need more humor, less dessert.
More writing, less walking around
brooding in my head.

September 7

*Overcast with high winds, white caps
on the lake, mid-70s*

The bear visited again, leaving
scat piles full of birdseed, dark
as the night she dropped them.
But she's becoming more
courteous, lifting the lid
on the storage seat, instead
of pitching the whole bench
into the yard; now she bends
the feeder's steel hook
(a 9/16 inch shepherd's rod)
gently to the garden floor
before mouthing the entire feeder.

September 8

Cool temps, mostly sun, with
puffed clouds in herds

Mental health improving
for everyone with a visit
from grandson, watching him
scamper, making a beeline
for the dock and a leap
into the cool lake shallows.

The grown-ups in his life
have issues . . . constant worry
and frustration over testing
and what results
might bring . . .

September 10

A cool, perfect September morning
The choppy lake blue under bluer skies

I finished my bicycle ride
in heavy, oncoming traffic.
(No fun pedaling through
a gravelly berm.) At home,
frustration recedes
with coffee on the patio.
My grandson feeds
zinnia petals into the jaws
of his Play-Doh dinosaur.
T-Rex sculpted in bright orange
and green, the petal-stuffed
mouth of this monster
humors my day.

September 12

Cindery skies with drizzle, low 70s

September rain and roses' roots
blossom, reaching viny fingers
through soil for nourishment.
Above the roots,
long stems, scraggly at summer's end,
hold buds and blooms five feet
above ground, poised
like cliff divers
before the long,
harrowing plunge
into turf.

September 14

Drab and sprinkling, low 70s

My 47th wedding anniversary today,
a tribute to patience and shared
expectations. Amid stability—
uncertainty: a family darkness
circles and threatens overhead.

Trying to ease worries, I pedal
against wind and rain, looking
like Oz's wicked witch, a tornado
of crows whirling above, bawling out
warnings, three caws at a time.

September 15

Crisp air, royal blue skies

At one end of 15 Mile, behind
civilized fencing, a trophy buck
notices me, raises regal eyes,
skull adorned with so many antlers
he appears to be wearing a shrub.
Brought to Legends Ranch
for stud services, his demeanor,
unflappable; he looks down
a perfect nose at me
humping my hooptie Trek past.

At the road's opposite end,
where farmers raise government hemp,
I am surprised by a three-year-old
Black Angus staring blankly
from behind an iron gate. Chewing
and slobbering over front hooves.
He, too, is unmoved by my passing.

One bound for sex and one
for steaks, it's clear my determined,
heart-healthy exercise
means nothing to animal neighbors,
simple and fit, bound
for their own nirvanas.

September 16

*Bright and breezy, temps
in the 60s*

Time is full of dead birds.
So why do we not see
roads and neighborhoods
littered with avian death?
Hunted and windshield
departures are obvious,
but what of the feathered shells
and skeletons of those
who age out and nose-dive
to earth? I have never
seen one simply drop
from the sky. Why?
Are there secret trees
in secret forests where millions
go to pass naturally and un-
noticed?

I must travel
to the afterlife
for an answer.

September 17

*Morning with full sun,
evening slate skies, 80*

I remember final words
on my father's memorial
bookmark: "I am waiting for you
in the sky." So, I may have
a traveling companion.
Familiar company's
a comforting thought
on my quest to know
the sacred resting place
of feathered souls.

September 20

*Murky morning but the sun
pushes through, a breezy 60*

Head full of storm clouds
and family turmoil:
after four years of love
and parenting, we get
dismal, unexpected
news, beginning on Friday
and grinding through
the weekend. Dour contrast
to the crisp blue weather
the world tried to show us
while our heads were lowered.

A vase full of sunflower
miniatures and zinnias
are bright, convivial guests
at the dinner table, but
we are having none of it.

September 21

Clear skies, cooling temps

Last day of summer season,
the cool-down and shorter days
lengthening shadows and hues;
pink-red and pale-yellow stippling
outer edges of trees.
The almanac says prepare
for a long winter, deep
with frigid cold.

We'll be eating green chili
over the weekend.

My dog is getting ready,
extending naps, curling on rugs
in sunny patches of light.
I am shaping up for falling temps
by following her example.

September 24

*Classic fall, high pressure,
cerulean blue skies and crisp temps*

Cortisone shot in my knee
this morning, then a long drive
south and east to Toledo.
Late afternoon, colors shifting
in trees and unharvested corn.
Husks browning in fields, dry
and aged before harvest.
Skin on my hands thinning
on top of the steering wheel,
wrinkled like mom and dad's.
Time passing through my hands.

September 25

*Cloudy rainy morning in Toledo,
temps in the low 50s*

Coffee and conversation
with a high school mate:
a couple of old toadstools
amongst a garden of busty dahlias—
waitresses jiggling their bacon
and hotcakes at Star Diner,
(and toadstools
with very big eyes).

September 28

*Clear morning, temps warming
into afternoon, 70s*

My son counts rings
of a felled Silver maple
and estimates seventy years.
An old squirrel's nest
cradled in the core
holds a fat, Brown Recluse
crawling groggily from his shelter.
Who poked his comfortable dream world?
What god or monster is deciding
how a spider's day will end?

With a four-year-old
dancing on top of cut logs
the outlook is grim
for a poisonous spider.

September 30

Cool and calm this morning, in 50s

Absent surface movement,
the lake is flat and breathless.
Trees filled with early color
double themselves in reflections
circling my pontoon deck.
Only disturbance: a soft
piano jazz
plinking a slow, smooth dance
over reflections in water.

October 1

*Clear and cool, Carolina blue,
morning in the 50s*

A light breeze today
pushes a red and silver rowboat
over the cove's water for fishing.
A huddled figure slouches
near the transom, his hat
pulled down to eyebrows.

So early, so still, I wonder
if he's sleeping,
anchored in a dream
by a drowning worm
squirming in weeds
near the bottom.

October 3

Foggy and cool, 60s

A breeze, east-south-east,
drags a blanket of wet fog
over the lake, further
dampening my sloshy thoughts.
Less zippy than a maple
changing color, I need a boost,
a face-slap charge
for paling energy.
A steaming shot of espresso
splashed down
and lashed across my soul.

October 4

*Misty rain, ground damp
and slippery, 60s*

Arming ourselves
for a custody battle,
we reach out
to a feisty, redheaded lawyer,
who peers at us over the top
of his half-rim glasses:
"Without standing," he says,
"You're pretty much fucked."
The sharp stick in the eye
makes it difficult
to say, "Thank you,
for your opinion."

October 5

*Gloomy skies early, but clouds
thinning to patches of blue, 64*

Songbirds have slipped away
and leaves pepper the lawn
with dots of autumn color.
Early morning insomnia
returned with worries
over my grandson's well-being.
At four he's old enough to know
his world's not right
and a hurt is growing.

Empty Adirondack chairs
resting near the fire pit
cradle a miniature Adirondack,
nested in their arms. Another
reminder of the little one
missing in our lives.

October 12

Steeped in my own foul weather

No writing for several days.
Loads of family trauma.
Someday, I will learn to dance
through upheaval,
but for now, it's all
I can do to tap my foot
in anger, doing my best
to avoid
spontaneous combustion.

October 13

Bright sun, light breeze, cool temps, 60s
Granville, OH

Perfect weather . . . October being
October. Bright sun bouncing off
the chrome trim of campers,
cream colors sharpened by light.
Toothy pumpkins and oversized
spiders haunt the lawns
of neighboring camp sites;
soup on the boil inside
tiny, temporary homes.

Tillie-dog
stretches on a cushy rug,
takes it all in, sun and warm
breeze drifting through her world.
Surrounded by a gleaming,
white fence in the distance,
a Dog-god has cordoned off
private space for her, and set out
a perfect, picnic day
for napping.

October 14

*Clear skies by noon,
temps in the 80s*

Way warm
for mid-October.
Local sparrows chipper,
bobbing in grass for insects.
Sun gathering
on shiny cricket backs;
sparrows feast all morning,
wondering if there's time
for another quick
mating dance
before the frost sets in.

October 17

*Clear, crisp, temps have nose-dived
Into the 40s*

Shocked into October
temps drop overnight.
Sparrows, playful in yesterday's
sunny grass, tuck themselves
into feathery puffballs
dangling from yew branches
and tips of spruce. Chestnut
brown and oyster gray
decorations, they hang
to celebrate Fall.

October 20

Second day after 10-hour drive,
Late rain, an achy 70 degrees

Tree-trunk shadows cross
the road in dark stripes,
and sunlight strobes the eyes
as I'm driving. A full day
of Fall's leafy dazzle.
But a bright, full moon
dominates insomnia,
haunted by more worry,
and a grandson
who's been pulled
from a family's
embrace.

October 24

Early sun, then silver haze,
temps in 30s

More driving, long miles ahead.
Prolonged sitting, hips stiffening,
old bones brittle as leaves
aging out on local oaks and maples.
I'm grinding it out at the wheel.

In mid-Michigan metal trees—
wind towers and turbines turn
24-hour shifts, electric food
for a hungry grid, while auto workers
slam-stamp parts through the night
or hover over sweaty grinders.
Products roll down the line;
my wheels rumble for home.

How much farther can it be?
How long can a night shift last?

October 26

November chill in October,
steel wool skies, high 30s, low 40s

Chainsaw and loppers
finally at rest. The burn pile
down to stray logs and leaves,
easy warm flames following
an afternoon of cutting
and lifting logs. I settle bones
and sore muscles into a lawn chair,
feet propped on a stump.

No boats, no lawnmowers,
no leaf blowers whining
around the lake. A fire's
pine crackling the only noise
gathered in a slight
and near-silent breeze.

Then a distant, metal chain tapping:
a skeletal finger on a flagpole
signaling,
"You
are not
alone."

October 27

*Early fog burning off, temps
warming by afternoon*

Waking this morning to four swans
lifting from the lake
through fog, rising and circling,
a mighty wind captured
under their wings, majestic
in flight. I wonder where
the little ones are?
Ones I saw yesterday, paddling
in safety, close behind them.

October 29

Wet everywhere, cool temps in 40s

Driving my son to the doctor
through a light gray drizzle,
black angus pepper a hillside,
their front hooves tucked beneath
the heft of dozing bodies,
rain collecting on broad backs.
It looks like Scotland, he tells me,
and, yes, it does. We're taking him
to address depression and anger
bubbling up and erupting in harmful
thoughts. He wants to go to the shed,
get the scythe, make hay of the ones
who brought this. His sadness,
deepening, weighing on him,
lead in the pockets of a man
treading water.

October 30

Early morning, patchy blue sky, colder
Crisp football Saturday weather

At night, numbers on the microwave's
digital clock hold lights out
for an old man wading
through darkness
to an urgent midnight meeting
in the bathroom.

Up this morning holding
down the fort (a worn, but
often used expression). I think
of Wittgenstein and how he showed us
the uncommunicated faith
we place in words. How tenuous,
invisible, but dependent, our meanings
and faith-based assumptions.
How dreamy our connections
to each other, our jobs,
the *idea* of a nation.

October 31

*Slate skies, occasional rain,
bone cold*

Halloween, my son's and his son's
favorite holiday. But this year
no children in costumes for us.
Our long and cheerless driveway
dark and empty.

November 1

Bright and nippy

All night the maple leaves
have fallen, drifting to new beds
in grass. It would be a shame
to move their curled husks
again, but the wind will
broom them along, like so many
homeless, struggling to brave
elements and officers
who only wish an ark
was available for sheltering.

November 2

Scattered cumulus with a bright
Simpson's blue background, 35

Election day for some,
outcomes twisting in the wind;
surgery day for others,
outcomes cradled
in a surgeon's hands,
scalpel (silver and still)
flat on a towel-covered tray.

Driving west to the hospital
sunrise began in cloud peaks
and dropped slowly
to earth, beginning
in treetops
       and sliding
              down leafy faces
hued with Michigan autumn,
the painted weather uplifting.

Politicians crowed and tried to take
credit. Then it started snowing.

November 3

Patchy clouds, 26 degrees

Up early before sunrise,
coffee in hand, sitting in bed,
Tillie pushes her head
under a free hand for petting.
Big morning surprise: a blanket
of snow over leaves, one
purple Clematis, the Weber grill
and a wheelbarrow
stationed near the fire pit.
Bird boxes, overnight, don
white stocking caps.

White against a white
background, swans on the lake
are ambushed by this
cold surprise.
Feeling less special, less
pompous, maybe (their long noses
lowered a bit) it's time to move
the Trumpeter family south,
where it might be warmer,
their pure white,
more appreciated.

November 4

Somber skies and cold, 29

Celebrating the last two
rosebuds, I scissor
and carry them inside
out of November's cold
to a vase of warm water.

They may open (tight little fists)
or they may not.

I hope to cajole blossoms
telling animal jokes
at the kitchen table,
where I have given them
pedestal-ed
front-row seating
for my ridiculous
standup routine.

November 5

*A sunny blue dome,
crisp and cool*

We have exiled our garden spirit,
our Bodhisattva in lotus position
carted into darkness
and protection in the shed.

Already I miss
his witness: his inward gaze
holding marigolds, sedum,
blazing star and Black-eyed Susans
under a shepherding presence.
His meditation turned now
to the shed's blank walls.

Outside a few late oak leaves,
rust and gold, detach
their hold on branches
and float through a river of air.

November 6

Early clouds, coolish,
warming later in the day

Four swans circling the lake,
low flying. A mountain range
of clouds behind them, sunrise pink.
Making an image idyllic
the best I can do sometimes . . .
frosting on a dog turd
when the rags of family relations
pile in a corner, rain-soaked
and soiled with grease.

November 11

Steady rain, temps in 40s

No poems for several days:
a personal desert for crossing,
at night . . . in mid-November.
A grave distance, I think.
Then an odor of leaves burning,
smoke from a smoldering fire pit
leads me forward; the scent
of a happy childhood, memories
worth rekindling.

November 17

Morning, a cool mist hanging,
no breeze

A flock of more than one hundred
Snow Geese circle
and settle in the lake:
an apparition, a snowdrift
on water. November's silence
broken suddenly by the traffic
of geese and high-pitched honking.
I laugh, imagining deer hunters,
hunkered down, wet and cold,
straining to hear a twig snap
from approaching deer.

Later, walking Tillie,
a slow, single gold leaf
twisted, rocked through air
and settled lightly on the ground.
From a distance, I thought it was
a bird . . . a magical, make-a-wish
for happiness one.

November 18

Ash gray skies, then snow, high 20s

A new snow blanket
illuminates the acre
leading out to the lake. I'm
waiting on a Beaver Moon, last
full moon during trapping season
when animal furs are thickest.

Because I don't trap,
beaver dams will interrupt
my dreams, my streams flooding
with blackwater sludge
during rains and hopes
for a family's early Spring.

November 19

Patchy clouds, bright sun, low 30s

Sun bursting through a week
of sullen clouds: an early Thanksgiving.
Everyone's happy: chickadees, titmice,
mourning doves picking their way
through leaf-scoops cupped with snow.
Three squirrels, fat as cats,
pounce on our loaded feeder;
birds scatter from the table,
leave the feast to greedy furballs
jamming their cheeks with seed.

November 21

Steady, strong winds, drizzle and cold

My new neighbor arrives with a friend
and both have guns. Deer season.
But after five days, no carcasses
hang from trees or drape
from a wooden trailer. No kill stories
to phone home. And I'm guessing
they're tired of drinking beer,
of sitting quietly in the wet cold,
of ice-rain sticking to caps
and shoulders, of fingers and hearts
growing numb, of deer
hiding in tangled thickets, patiently
holding positions, nearly invisible
through the hunters' freezing eyelids.

November 24

More wind, sunny and cold

I've raked leaves
two and three times, but
wind keeps pushing them
into crannies
where I'll either strain my back
reaching for them or just
throw my hands up, defeated.
My compulsive raking's a joke,
like a chicken wire fence
against pesky, thieving coons.
The leaves' dry laughter
skitters into the woods.

November 25

Slate skies and drizzle, 43

A damp Thanksgiving
without a grandson.
His absence poking us,
a boney finger
jabbed at our hearts.
Difficult to accept blessings
and "thankfulness"
as spirit of the day.

November 28–30

*Gray, gray, gray, and snow
piling up, low teens overnight*

Surrounded by a lake, a creek,
and acres of snow, water
comforts and completes me,
invites me to embrace
its slow gurgling voice
tumbling over rocks, whispering
to my own body's water,
asking for a dance—
a slow one,
back to wider,
deeper waters
before hard winter
and the stillness of ice.

December 2

Powder blue skies, warming temps, 40s

Awake at night
to a house so quiet
I can hear blood
pulsing in my ears.

The drip of snowmelt
into metal eaves—
a carpenter's fitful tapping
to a restless insomniac.

December 7

Snow with ice, 14 degrees

The car is sleeping
under a blanket of snow,
an ice sheet pulled up
over its windshield.
A bright red bow
on a Christmas wreath
hangs on the barn door—
a beacon for package drivers
delivering to our home:
*Never mind
the blinding snow,* it says,
over here, over here.

December 8

Stiffening cold, low 20s all day

Reading inside. How fine
to finish a novel at sunset,
serendipitously.
With a deep snow backdrop
perfect for hunting,
a Red-tailed hawk
perches in lakeside oaks.
Our swans could not
care less, casually
dunking their heads
into freezing water,
warmer than surrounding air,
unthreatened by weather
or the screech of a menacing hawk.

December 10

Spotty sunshine, warming to 30s

Puttering with television
connections and internet,
then finances, electric motors
and bird feeders.
Nothing satisfies.
I squirm like an animal
in a too-small cage.
Cabin fever . . .
restlessness
leashed to an indoor stake.

December 16

High winds, dreary skies, 40s

Gale force winds roaring
through empty branches, some
log-thick and broken away,
scatter over roof and yard.
I sit up all night with tall oaks,
praying they hold ground,
winds swirling wildly overhead.

In morning light,
sudden power gusts
blast and shred
my trailer's canvas;
in tatters it snaps
like a circus whip.
Our hanging bird feeder
swings wildly in place—
a terrified chimp.

December 17

More cold, more gray

I've spent the night tossing
coins in a phantom fountain
hoping to bring sleep
with mindless repetition . . .
but no relief
from thoughts of a five-year-old,
his spirit entangled
with loss and confusion,
and no escape
from family bedlam.

His sorrow haunts me.
It's like sliding down
a rescue rope,
escaping safely at the bottom,
listening all the while
to howls of a family pet
trapped in a room above,
flames crawling up the building.

December 18

High pressure, cobalt skies, 28

Overnight the wind slips
out of Michigan, leaving morning
full of quiet sunshine. Unusual
chirping outside my window
mid-December, when songbirds
are generally long gone. So
who's this feathery Sinatra?

Given a little sunshine
and warmer temps, the path
to a cheerful song
is clearing,
melting winter
cold in our hearts.

December 19

Dingy gray and cold, no wind

More annoying than constant cold
and a smothering blanket
of clouds—no songbirds
since yesterday's sudden outburst!
Their songs' absence a sinking
dampness more unsettling
than sleeping in a morgue.

With a grandson
missing for Christmas,
we scratch our way
toward light and joy
hoping to find purchase
in seasonal trappings
and tidings of good cheer.

December 21

Solstice, brittle cold, low 20s

Walking dirt roads with the dog,
I pass through woods
near the cemetery
where I wished
to bury my parents' ashes
this summer, but the headstone,
delayed by Covid backorders,
arrived too late in November.

I could not muster the will
to set them underground
when earth was freezing over,
remembering how they hated
cold, and moved to Arizona.

December 24

In Columbus for Christmas,
weather bright and mild

Green chili with carnitas
for breakfast; ham with mac
and cheese for dinner; open mouths
for cookies and chocolates
whenever. Rooms of light
and laughter, my daughter
and son together for Christmas,
first time after many years.
We pool our joys and refresh
memories, restocking our shelves
for cold months ahead.

December 26

Occasional rain, mild temps, low 50s

On an early walk
sparrows and wrens hopping,
weaving between branches
of bordering shrubs. On this path,
more than four hundred miles
south of home, I hear
three birds I know:
nuthatch, titmouse, and screeches
from a Red-tailed hawk.
These States are large,
with weather unpredictable,
but the sounds of home
travel well.

December 27

Again, temps mild with light rain
in Columbus area

Final days of a year pockmarked
by insect pests and virus; our daily lives
directed by organisms so small
they rival the number of devils
dancing on a pencil point.

A death-web wrapped
around the globe, the virus
will snare more lives next year,
maybe mine; but like the prodigal son's
father, I am focused on the one
who needs love most,
and how he might return.

December 31

*Several days of drizzle, moderate temps,
but drab, drab, drab*

Short days after Christmas—
time to take my foot off
the accelerator. No more
barreling through to-do lists,
requisite parties with friends,
sit-down dinners with the family's
many faces.

Longer walks and exercise
with the dog. Pleased
with the attention,
she prances along, peeking
over her shoulder,
checking to see
if I'm *really here* . . .
in the moment,

and a smile
is what I give her.

About the Author

Alan Basting was born in Detroit and grew up in northwest Ohio. He attended Earlham College and received an undergraduate degree from the University of Cincinnati. He earned graduate degrees from Colorado State University (MA) and Bowling Green State University (MFA), and taught creative writing, composition, and literature at University of Cincinnati and Owens Community College in Toledo.

His books and chapbooks include: *Singing from the Abdomen* (Stone-Marrow Press, 1976), *What the Barns Breathe* (Window Press, 1982), *Suddenly, Herons* (The Writer's Cooperative of Toledo, 1986), *Deep Time, Daily Habits and Events* (sponsored by The Arts Commission of Toledo, 1992), *Nothing Very Sudden Happens Here* (Lynx House Press, 2013), *Home and Away* (Finishing Line Press, 2019) *Apples and Crows* (Kelsay Books, 2023), and *White Fence: an Ekphrastic Collaboration* (Window Press, 2024).

Alan and his wife, Cassie, reside in Lilley, Michigan, in the middle of the Manistee National Forest near the village of Bitely.

More information regarding Alan and his poetry can be found at: alanbastingpoetry.com

www.ingramcontent.com/pod-product-compliance
Lightning Source LLC
Chambersburg PA
CBHW022014160426
43197CB00007B/433